Conversations
With
The Most High

A Book Of
Testimonial Poems

Bianca Avanti Rinehart

Copyright © 2024 Bianca Avanti Rinehart

All rights reserved. No part of this book may be used or reproduced in any manner without written permission of the copyright owner except for the use of quotations in a book review.

Published by Kellie Kelly World Publishing ®
Edited by Kellie Kelly World Publishing ®
Connect With Us on Instagram: @KellieKellyWorld
Cover Design by Kelli Ryan

"Keep on asking, and you will receive what you ask for. Keep on seeking, and you will find. Keep on knocking, and the door will be opened to you.
Matthew 7:7

Contents

PART ONE: EXPOSED 7
    Pretending To Be Me 12
    We Are Sinners 17
    The Great Deceiver 22
    Imperfect 25
    Come Out, In Jesus Name 28

PART TWO: GOD REPLIES 30
    Little Girl 38
    Focus on Me 40
    Father 42
    I am 44
    Taste And See 46
    Present 49
    The Lord Will Provide 51
    Jericho 53

ABOUT BIANCA AVANTI RINEHART 55

Dedication

This book of testimonial poems is dedicated to Michael—whom I met in a fleeting moment, yet your words lingered, a whisper from God's heart to mine. You poured life into me, spoke a truth that stirred my spirit, reminding me of a purpose I had yet to see. You saw me when others turned away, lifted me when I was low, and ignited a fire for Christ I didn't know was waiting to burn. You are heaven's messenger, a blessing I carry always.

Part One: Exposed

As a child, I was full of fire, spinning in circles until sweat drenched my skin, and chasing daylight until the stars came out to play. I'd push myself to the brink, lungs burning, relying on two sharp puffs of albuterol to keep my body moving. But when night came, there was nowhere to run. My mother had chosen drugs over me, vanishing into a world where I didn't matter. My father had drifted away like autumn leaves before my heart could learn the shape of his shadow. My skin was too dark for his pride, rejected not for who I was, but for the color of my soul's shell.

And the wounds of molestation left by the very people who should've protected me—they cut the deepest, piercing the parts of me where no hand could reach. Every time I stepped through that front door, the truth struck like a heavy blow—home, that sacred place, had become a battlefield of endless sorrow, a place of unrelenting heartache.

My grandparents drowned their sorrows in bottles and brawls until sleep took them. They gave what little they could though their brokenness which fed the darkness inside me. Their traumas, like rain on bitter seeds, nurtured the weeds of rejection, abandonment, and perverted, twisted love. These roots took hold in my soul, leaving me feeling like a passing shadow, unseen and never enough. Anger festered where tenderness should have bloomed, and the weight of their pain silenced my voice before it ever had the chance to rise and soar.

At twelve, I wove myself a cloak of lies, a false identity to shield my tender soul from the world's jagged edges. I became someone else, hiding in the shadows of deceit, letting the darkness wrap around me like a lover, whispering false promises of power and safety. I walked tall, wore the mask of a man, strong and untouchable—but no matter how long I wore that disguise, I was still a girl beneath, fragile and afraid. I played the part of toughness, thinking it would keep me safe, but deep inside, I was a frightened child, trembling under the weight of the very men who sought to pierce through my illusion. Yet if I hid, I believed I was in control, untouchable, no longer prey to the pain that once broke me. But in truth, the hiding only imprisoned me, the walls I built becoming my own chains.

Surrounded by the shadows of death, illness, and poverty, I found myself bound in a relentless cycle—pulled through the doors of juvenile facilities, mental institutions, group homes, and the clutches of addiction. By 2015, I had hit the jagged rock bottom. Desperate and broken, I cried out to God, pleading for deliverance. That cry ignited a flicker of light within me, sparking a spiritual odyssey. Down the winding rabbit hole I went, searching for salvation in places I had never dared to look before. I embraced veganism, sought stillness in meditation, stretched my body in yoga, and swam through the depths of New Age philosophies. Mornings found me clinging to the words of Abraham Hicks, hoping to bend the universe to my will, to manifest the life I longed for. I wrote affirmations with trembling hands, attended sound baths to heal the wounds deep within, aligning my chakras like steppingstones to peace. I even sat in the sanctuary of Agape, where voices spoke of Christ Consciousness and the law of attraction, offering new words to old prayers.

In the wake of this vibrant awakening, I felt a surge of energy coursing through my veins, a fierce readiness to embrace life's wild dance. Yet, the high was fleeting, like a mirage dissolving in the desert sun, leaving me hollow, a vessel without a purpose. I sensed the discord within me, an echo of yearning that urged me to seek something deeper, something more.

Then came 2020, a year of solitude, a rarity in my whirlwind existence, where I had always spun from one relationship to the next, never stopping long enough to breathe. It is said that when God calls you into the silence of your own company, He opens the door to your soul and truly reaches you. As the world pressed pause due to the pandemic and the cacophony of life fell silent, clarity washed over me like a cleansing rain. In that stillness, the truth emerged from the shadows, illuminating the truth I had been too busy to see.

In that fleeting moment, I was caught in the dance of flirtation with a woman, my heart a mosaic of uncertainty. Then, one day, I dared to whisper my truth—questioning my own desires, contemplating the words of the Bible. Her reaction struck me like a thunderclap; she dismissed the Bible as a relic of the past, twisted and rewritten. The abrupt change in her demeanor left me reeling, a shockwave of emotions crashing through me.

In that charged silence, I felt an undeniable pull to explore, to seek answers in the very scriptures she scorned. As I delved into the pages, I discovered Genesis 2:24, a verse that spoke of a man leaving his parents to unite with his wife, becoming one flesh, and Genesis 1:27, where the divine hand-crafted humanity in His image, male and female. In that sacred revelation, clarity pierced the fog of confusion—I knew I had to sever the ties that bound us.

After we hung up, I was enveloped by a tide of repentance, the weight of my choices crashing down like waves upon the shore. In that stillness, I faced the truth within me, a reckoning that would guide my path forward.

In the midst of my turmoil, I had a profound encounter with Jesus, a moment that pulled back the veil of my existence. My life unfolded before me like a flickering film, revealing the raw, jagged edges of my soul—the ugliness I had tried so hard to hide, the hardened places I thought I could escape. A tempest of emotions surged within me—guilt and love intertwined, shame and freedom danced in a bittersweet embrace.

For years, I had wielded the pen as my sword, using writing to lay bare my truth, to vent frustrations, to celebrate the small victories that flickered like stars in my darkest nights. In those pages, my pain transformed into a blazing passion, igniting a fire that poured forth as poetry. Words became my sanctuary, each line a testament to the battles fought and the resilience found in the ashes of my struggles. I began to weave my heartache into something beautiful, a tapestry of hope rising from the depths of despair.

As a new believer, I wandered the landscape of my faith, alone in a world that felt both vast and unwelcoming. Without the embrace of fellow believers, I continued grappling with the heavy chains of childhood wounds, caught in a relentless struggle against sin and the flesh that clung to me like a second skin. God had only begun to stir within me, and I found myself ensnared in a tempest of spiritual warfare, facing my personal demons with trembling courage.

At the forefront loomed the specter of perversion, a deep-seated affliction that had borne a harvest of bitter fruit through the years. Yet as I journeyed through this dark night of the soul, clarity began to seep into the cracks of my confusion. I started to unveil the lies woven by the enemy, the deceptions I had clung to for too long, and the falsehoods that had dictated my every move. With each revelation, I peeled back the layers of my past, confronting the darkness with the light of newfound truth, igniting a fierce desire for liberation and healing.

Pretending To Be Me

I sit here low, close to the earth
Life's weight heavy on my spirit, pressed deep into the dirt.
I have been shattered, stripped, and torn,
My soul laid bare, no soft place to land, no peace, no shore.

The only witness to my heart's cry,
Is the one I've wronged, lying close by,
And I have no friends, for I've hidden away,
The truest me, the one who could sway
Mountains,
The one who knows her will is steel,
Who knows her spirit cannot kneel.

Yet when I stand in the crowd's cold light,
That fire dims, shrinks from sight.
She's buried deep, yet still she calls,
A whisper beneath the world's great walls.

Someday she'll rise, someday she'll soar,
For strength is boundless, though it's worn.

And *poof*, in steps this counterfeit soul,
Bold and brazen, she struts on parade,

Conversations With The Most High

Unafraid, untouched, and ever unbothered,
Pretending life's breeze has never been weighed.

With her painted grin, she steals the stage,
All light and joy—a hollow disguise.
So the world only sees her dazzling lie,
Never glimpsing the me tucked away inside.

But this true heart beats hard, aching to be known,
While the mask whispers low, "This stage is mine,
I've been here, darling, reigning in style,
There's no room for truth; it's my time to shine."

She mocks the struggle, the scars, the fight,
A borrowed grace draped over my light.
But I'll rise from this pretense, one day to be free,
For the real me, fierce and proud, is destined to see.

Yes, I scream, a cry from the soul!
"Please, let me rise, I'm weary of this role."
Down here in the shadows, gasping for air,
Living in fear while you dance without care.

I've touched the light, felt its heat on my skin,
Known the power when truth lets me in.
When honesty blooms, hearts open wide,
But you—you've played the part, cast me aside.

So now, step back, give me my space,
For I am the strength, the courage, the grace.
You may be a piece, a page in my past,
But I no longer need to hide behind that mask.

Those painted smiles, those scripted lines—
Enough of the charades, the endless confines.

Conversations With The Most High

I'm stepping forward, fierce and unbound,
No more whispers, no more chains around.

Oh, you've experienced too much, walked through fires I couldn't touch,
And that strength in you, that raw, unfiltered truth—
It shakes me, makes me small,
Makes me wonder if I ever was anything at all.

For if you step forward, fierce and unchained,
Who am I? A shadow fading, a ghost unnamed.
Who will I charm, who will still seek me out,
If they see your soul, your light—no doubt?

I was there when the hurt was too deep to bear,
I played the part, a shield, a mask, kept watch over your despair.
Every day I kept you safe, hid you from their eyes,
Yet here you stand, calling me a lie.

Ungrateful, that's what you are,
As if I didn't carry you when life left scars.
I shared your light, gave you your days,
Now you say it's my time to fade away?

But I know, deep down, my time is thin—
You are ready to rise, to let truth begin.
So go, let them see you, raw and real,
And I will vanish as you heal.

Yes, I've had enough.
You—yes, you—have carved wounds deep,
Hurt the ones I loved, stripped my spirit bare,
And left me friendless, alone in the dark.

Conversations With The Most High

All this time, you whispered soft lies,
Told me I was small, too raw, too weak,
Said I'd be judged, said they'd leave,
And I believed, held myself back, too afraid to breathe.

You painted my soul in your shadows, hid me away,
Made me a stranger to those who would stay.
No real friends, no bonds that could last—
You locked me out, kept me shackled to your past.

But now I see you, see through the game,
All your pretense, all your need for fame.
You lied to me, starved me of love and light,
Pushed the good away, held tight in spite.

It was your ego, your pride, your desire to be seen,
That stole from me all that could have been.
But no more—I'm stepping into the sun,
Leaving you behind as I become one.

I have people to meet, new worlds to greet,
And I'll do it all as me, as I am,
Not the mask you wore, not the lies you spun,
Not the games you played under a borrowed sun.

You told them tales, whispered false vows,
Said you wanted them close, promised them love,
But it was empty talk to feed your need,
All a show to satisfy a fleeting greed.

And when the curtain fell, when truth called your bluff,
I'd step in, heart heavy, cleaning up the dust.
Picking up pieces you shattered with ease,
Breaking hearts you never cared to keep.

Conversations With The Most High

But I'm done now, through with this charade.
I've tasted love—the kind that stays.
It's a fire within, no longer a spark,
And I see you now, a hollow, running dark.

You're out of fuel, all smoke and show,
While I'm finding my way, learning to glow.
The light is near, I feel its pull—
This strength is mine, full and whole.

Here's my farewell, a goodbye for good,
For I'm stepping out, as I always should.

We Are Sinners

I am no better, no higher, no purer
Than any soul walking this earth.
We are sinners, each of us, born of this nature,
Each needing a savior to cleanse our hurt.

Deliverance, yes—deliverance from this sexual craving,
This wild hunger that knows no name.
I never called myself a lesbian, no label to bear,
Just a free spirit, drifting, lost in the flames,
Following pleasure, chasing the thrill,
Moving through bodies, but empty still.

Yes, we are sinners, all broken and bent,
But tell me, whose sin has weighed me down so low?
Whose hands laid these burdens upon my soul?
I search for meaning, for truth that won't flee,
Yet here I am, tangled in webs of lost identity,
With brokenness spilling from my veins,
A heart full of questions, a mind wracked in pain.

Who am I beneath this mask, this disguise?
A sinner, yes, but searching, with hope in my eyes.

9 years old, my girl cousin
Wanted to playhouse

Conversations With The Most High

In my closet we hid
You be daddy, she says.
Get on top of me
Go up and down
My aunt busted open the door
Acted a straight clown

10 years old, my boy cousin
Wanted me to touch his penis
While our grandparents were asleep
Shh, he says
As he puts the covers over our heads
We are sinners

I grew older, a slave to sin, bound tight,
Became the man in the love I sought,
Grasping for control, playing the part,
Holding all the cards close to my heart.

I chased women as broken as me,
Their wounds like mirrors, reflections I could see.
We clung to each other in shadows and pain,
Two or more souls lost, tangled in shame.

Daddy gone, nothing but a hollow space,
Mama deep in her haze, lost to the taste—
Grandparents, their bottles drained each night,
And me, small and afraid, aching for light.

Who would shield me, keep me safe?
Where was my refuge, my sacred place?

But no hands reached out, no love came near,
So I learned to harden, bury my fear.
Yes, I was a child in need, but the world was blind,
Left to find my way, to break or to bind.

Conversations With The Most High

So here I stand, a testament of scarred grace,
Longing to heal, to reclaim my place.

We are sinners, all of us,
Hungry to be seen, even in our dust and lust,
Grasping for a way to make this brokenness fit,
Justifying the lives we chose to live—
Lies from hell, burning from the pit.

Oh, Satan knows his craft well,
Spins confusion like a dark spell,
And we, we were just children then,
Pulled too soon into a world of sin.

Our voices hushed and stilled,
A silence we wore like armor, a shield,
Left to guard our own tender hearts,
Playing parts we didn't yet understand.

So we built images to bury the shame,
Took on faces that masked the pain,
Played the man in a play we never chose,
Hiding the wounds no one ever knows.

Yes, we are sinners, craving to belong,
Yet trapped in shadows, singing sorrow's song.

Cheating, lusting, weaving webs of deceit,
Using women as sexual idols, my flesh at their feet.
I moved from altar to altar,
A wanderer lost, a soul turned to stone,
Masturbating to feed an insatiable hunger,
An empty shell, just a voice without a home,
Screaming for help, but too proud to cry,
Too lost in the chaos to ever ask why.

Conversations With The Most High

How many times did I don that false guise,
Wearing a mask, believing the lies?
So many times, of wearing a fake penis
I started to believe; this is who I am
I started to believe this façade was my truth,
Not seeing the broken child, the lost youth,
Not knowing that I was a sinner by nature,
Chained to desires that twisted my features.

Yet inside, the heartbeat—a desperate plea,
Yearning for love, for a chance to be free.
I walked in the shadows, searching for light,
A flicker of hope in the depths of the night.

This is no excuse for the choices I've made,
No matter how I twist the words,
No matter how I strive to justify the pain,
To come to my own defense in this tangled charade.

Our society sings praises for wicked ways,
Celebrates the darkness, cloaked in disguise.
Oh, please, God, reach down, help us see,
For in this deception, we're dying inside.

We are sinners, lost in the shadows,
Hungry for redemption, aching for grace.
We need a savior, a light in the storm,
His name is Jesus, pure in form.

A man who knew no sin, walked in the light,
The ultimate sacrifice, shining so bright.
In His embrace, we find our way home,
Through the ashes of shame, no longer alone.

Paying the fine for our debts,
The wages of sin, oh, they weigh heavy,

Conversations With The Most High

Death hanging like a dark cloud over our heads,
Yet He died the death we so rightfully feared,
It is finished—He is the risen King,
The promise of hope in a world so seared.
He offers us a chance, a lifeline so pure,
To live with Him, eternally secure.
For His yoke is easy, His burden is light,
He walks with the weary, bringing strength to the fight.
He is not a man, no, that He should not lie,
There's truth in His arms, His love as our anchor, as in Him we abide.

The same way He delivered me from shadows and chains,
He can reach you, too, and completely erase your pains.
We are all sinners, His grace knows no bounds,
In His mercy, a melody of hope resounds.

Repent, believe in the gospel's sweet song,
And find in His love where you truly belong.
So, lift up your heart, let the chains fall away,
For in Him, dear soul, there's a brand-new day.
Amen.

The Great Deceiver

Three a.m., the witching hour,
Your game is exposed, your shadows unfurl.

You whisper deceit, hoping to sting,
Holding me only by a fragile little string.

You can't reach me in the light of day,
So you creep in my dreams, where shadows play,
Programming my subconscious with venomous lies,
Preying on the spiritually weak, where God's lost sheep cries.

Oh, I see you, you who cast your spells,
Witches, warlocks, and demons—
I know all too well.
You lurk in the corners, where darkness can thrive,
But I stand unbroken, determined to survive.

For I am no victim, no pawn in your game,
With the light of the Spirit, I call you by name.
So come forth, if you dare, and try your best,
But know this, I rise, I will not rest.

Conversations With The Most High

Get behind me, Satan, you great deceiver,
For I am protected, covered in the sweet blood of Jesus.
Set me free from these chains that bind,
For I am ready to leave the past behind.
With strength anew, I'll rise and soar,
Breaking the weight, I'll be bound no more.

The battle I fight is not of flesh and bone,
No, warfare is spiritual, where the heart finds its tone.
It's not mere bodies that I wrestle against,
But principalities, lurking in shadows, intense.

Against powers unseen, against rulers of night,
I stand on the promise of His love and His light.
3 a.m. finds me, and the war drums resound,
Surrounded by darkness, yet in faith, I am found.

I need some ammo, a weapon of grace,
God bless my soul as I take my place.
For with every prayer, every cry to the skies,
I reclaim my power; in His name, I will rise.

So, take the helmet of salvation,
The sword of the Spirit, a light in the dark,
The Word of the living God, igniting the spark.

I speak against all your deceit,
Against the lies that you weave,
Your game is weak, and time is up—
The victory is already won, the real truth that we must believe.

You mislead God's people with plots of pure evil,
But I rise to expose you, unravel your sequel.

Awakening from slumber, we stand tall and proud,
Putting on the full armor, our voices raised out
oud. unbowed.

For the weapons of this warfare are not of the flesh or carnal,
But mighty through God, for the pulling down of strongholds.

Stay strapped, my soul, for the battle is near,
In these 3 a.m. battlegrounds, we conquer our fear.
With faith as our shield and love as our guide,
We march forth as warriors, with God by our side.

Imperfect

Lord, deal with me, for my heart is torn,
Why do I give in when I know what I've sworn?
I stand firm in my word, a fortress of light,
Yet temptation slips in, shrouded in night.

It shows itself boldly, in countless forms,
A whisper in shadows, as my flesh warms.
I left my door cracked, a vulnerable plea,
And now I wrestle with the storm inside me.

I tell you I am celibate, a vow I hold dear,
But still, you persist, like a shadow drawing near.

Why won't you just leave me, let my heart be free?
You creep in with seduction, taunting my dignity.

What begins as a touch, a simple embrace,
Turns into temptation that I can't quite face.
A massage that morphs into oral sex,
I battle the guilt, trying hard not to weep over what may come next.

Lord, help me to stand, to guard what is mine,
To turn from temptation, to seek the divine.

For in the quiet moments, when the shadows draw near,
I yearn for Your strength, to banish my fear.

Please, don't.
Let's simply be present, in this moment shared,
Yet inside, you roar like a lion, fierce and I am completely unprepared.
I stand here, a lioness, strong yet torn,
A recovering sex addict, in this battle reborn.

I see you,
You can't hide from me, no shadow too deep,
I know your deepest desires, the secrets you keep.
Feels good, doesn't it, this dance on the edge?
But I feel the weight of temptation's cruel pledge.

Do you smell the snitch on my clothes, that old, haunting scent?
This aroma clings to me, a residue of lament.
A stain that won't come out, no matter how I try,
A reminder of battles fought and lost, of nights I can't deny.

Yet here I stand, resolute in my fight,
With every breath, I reclaim my light.
So please, don't. Let's find peace in our place,
For I am a lioness, reclaiming my grace.

70 days,
No masturbation, no fornication,
Just me and Jesus, walking through this path of temptation.
Yet I stumbled, I faltered, in the silence I wailed,

As the shadows whispered secrets, and my resolve unveiled.

So here we are,
Am I baring my scars?
Understand, I'm not mad at you, my dear,
But at myself, for the choices I fear.
Looking in the mirror, the truth comes alive,
I see just how imperfect, how I struggle to thrive.
Each mark tells a story, each flaw a refrain,
A testament of battles, of joy and of pain.

But I rise from the ashes, I gather my grace,
For in these very scars, I find my place.
I am a work in progress, a soul in the light,
With Jesus beside me, I'll continue and win the fight.

Come Out, In Jesus Name

They find delight in shadows,
In the dark dance of demonic rituals,
Woe to those who twist the truth,
Calling good evil, and evil good.
Continue in your ways,
But know this: you are puppets,
Strings pulled by spirits unseen.

Oh, hear the call!
Come out, in the name of Jesus!
Let the light break through your chains,
For freedom awaits beyond the veil,
Where love conquers all,
And the soul can breathe again.

As the beat drops, a spell unfolds,
All eyes drawn in, captivated by the false light.
Oh, Satan, your charm is a snare,
A sweet deception that leads to demise.
You may feel good now, basking in the thrill,
But know that shadows linger,
And suffering waits just beyond the bright facade.

One more tequila shot, one more puff,
Promises of escape, yet they choke out your life.

They won't save you from the storm that's to come.
Hear the call!
Come out, in the name of Jesus!
For the truth is a beacon,
And freedom, my dear, is your birthright.

Discrediting the Bible,
Declaring it old news,
Twisting its sacred words,
Turning truth into lies,
A dangerous game played by the unrepentant.

Manipulating the masses,
Wolves draped in sheep's clothing,
But behold, God is rising,
Calling forth His true church,
The faithful who stand firm in the light.

He is separating the wheat from the tares,
Drawing a line through the shadows,
For His truth is a clarion call,
A force that cannot be silenced.
Let those who seek Him awaken,
For the dawn of justice is at hand,
And hope will rise, unyielding and strong.

And you evil ones will reap, what you sow
Come out, in Jesus name!

Part Two: God Replies

I have turned away from the shadows, letting go of all the ties that once bound me. No more entanglements with women, no more whispers of witchcraft haunting my days. For months, I have walked this path of clarity, abstaining from masturbation and releasing the weed that clouded my mind. In this sacred silence, I found the heartbeat of God, His presence wrapping around me like a warm embrace. In the stillness, I felt Him draw near, a deep closeness igniting within me. Dreams—prophetic dreams—began to unfold, though their significance eluded me at first. In one of these dreams, Jesus stood before me, radiant yet unrecognized, speaking truth in the streets. A crowd gathered, entranced by His words, yet blind to the miracle among them. They did not see the light shining so brightly, the Savior walking among us, calling us from our slumber. As I stood witness to His grace, my heart surged with passion, knowing that His message is alive and we are beckoned to awaken, to see with new eyes and listen with open hearts.

In that dream, I was enveloped in a knowing, an unmistakable truth—it was Jesus before me. Tall and slender, adorned in a flowing white robe that seemed to shimmer with light, He radiated a presence that transcended the ordinary. Drawn closer, I reached out to touch Him, and when our hands met, I was struck by the warmth of His bronze skin, a hue rich and radiant, unlike anything I had ever known. His voice, gentle yet powerful, echoed in my heart: "I will not come as people have pictured me." Overwhelmed by the weight of this revelation, I fell to His feet, my spirit laid bare, weeping as though my very soul was being unburdened. He knelt beside me, a comforter in my despair, as tears flowed freely, a river of raw emotion washing over me. In that moment, peace wrapped around my heart like a warm embrace, but fear also stirred within me, a haunting realization that many may miss His coming. They wait for a figure cloaked in the familiar, blinded by their own expectations, while the truth stands right before them— unrecognized, yet eternally present. This dream ignited a fire within me, a passionate call to awaken those who sleep, to open their eyes and see the divine in the everyday, for He is among us, beckoning us to recognize Him anew.

This dream washed over me with a force that felt as if God Himself were whispering directly into my soul, a sacred dialogue that demanded to be heard. I sat with fervor, my pen dancing across the page, diligently capturing every word, every revelation, as if they were threads of divine wisdom woven just for me. In those moments, as a new believer, I tasted the essence of what it truly means to walk with God—stripped bare of the world's clamor, I found myself cradled in His presence, a sanctuary of peace and grace. It was a beautiful experience, yet a pang of loneliness echoed within me. I was unaccustomed to this solitude, a stark contrast to the relationships and endless busyness that once filled my days.

Here, in this sacred stillness, I discovered a new rhythm of living, one that revolved around the simplicity of waking up, praying fervently, worshiping with every fiber of my being, crying out my fears and hopes, writing my heart's deepest cries, then surrendering to sleep, only to awaken and repeat this sacred cycle. For months, I immersed myself in this newfound way of being, and though the beauty of my communion with God shone brightly, I often felt the ache of absence—the longing for human connection amidst the profound intimacy I shared with the Divine. In this delicate dance between solitude and connection, I learned to embrace the beauty of being alone with God, knowing that even in loneliness, I was never truly abandoned.

In the midst of this profound beauty, I was thrust into a battle that raged within the very depths of my soul—a spiritual warfare so intense it felt like a storm crashing against the fragile shores of my newfound faith. I found myself grappling with forces I could scarcely comprehend, and though I didn't yet know how to fight back, I clung desperately to the name of Jesus, that sacred name, like a lifeline in the tempest. Dark and twisted dreams haunted my nights, while demons lurked in the shadows, eager to lead me astray. Seduction whispered from every corner, as women, embodiments of temptation, sought to ensnare me in their alluring grasp.

Sleep paralysis gripped me in its icy hold, leaving me trapped between worlds, a prisoner of my own mind. It was in these harrowing moments that the truth of Ephesians 6:12 pierced through the fog of my confusion: *we wrestle not against flesh and blood, but against principalities, against powers, against the rulers of darkness of this world, against spiritual wickedness in high places*. This revelation became my battle cry, echoing in the chambers of my heart, reminding me that the fight was not merely against the tangible but against the very essence of evil that sought to extinguish the light within me.

With every trial, I grew more resolute, understanding that my journey was not just one of personal salvation but a fierce stand against the darkness that enveloped our world. I may have been shaken, but in that shaking, I found strength; in my vulnerability, I discovered resilience. I was learning, step by step, that even in the fiercest of battles, I was never alone, for the name of Jesus would be my shield and my sword, illuminating the path toward victory.

In the throes of an aching loneliness, I found myself kneeling before the heavens, my heart laid bare before God, pleading for a man to enter my life, a companion who would affirm the woman I yearned to be—the woman He said I was. With trembling hands, I began to etch on paper the qualities I longed for in a partner, my desires flowing like a river uncontained. Yet, deep within, I knew my intentions were tainted, not pure; I was not merely seeking love, but rather a balm for my wounded soul, a salve for the gaping emptiness that echoed within me.

I sought to fill the cracks in my spirit, to piece together a life that felt fragmented and hollow. In my heart of hearts, I believed that marrying a man would somehow complete me, that he would be the missing piece to my puzzle, the final stroke of brilliance on a canvas marred by sorrow and struggle. I longed for validation, to be seen and cherished, to escape the solitude that clung to me like a heavy cloak.

But in my quest for wholeness, I overlooked a profound truth: that completeness cannot be found in another person, but within oneself. As I poured my desires onto the page, I was still haunted by the shadow of my brokenness, unaware that true fulfillment begins with self-love, with embracing the essence of who I am, unfiltered and unapologetic. In my fervent search for love, I was called to recognize that before I could find a partner, I first needed to mend the heart within me, to rise from the ashes of loneliness and reclaim my own worthiness, for I was already a masterpiece, beautifully crafted by the hands of the Divine.

As I knelt in prayer, my heart yearning for a husband, the shadows of the enemy slithered into my life, wrapping themselves around my hopes and dreams. Men emerged from the corners of my existence, their voices smooth as silk, professing interest in me, declaring themselves spiritual souls—yet their roots were not grounded in the sturdy soil of biblical truth. Oh, how they spoke the language of faith, weaving words that felt familiar, comforting, like a warm breeze on a summer day, but deep down, I sensed a dissonance, a fragile facade.

In my eagerness not to miss the chance at love, I opened myself to their advances, believing that to remain receptive was to invite possibility. My resolute "no's," once a fierce shield, began to tremble and falter, morphing into hesitant "maybe's." Each small surrender took me further down a treacherous path—a slippery slope of repeated sexual sin. I became like an open door, a welcoming invitation for those who sought not to cherish my spirit but to exploit my vulnerability.

With each encounter, I felt my essence erode, the light within me dimming as I allowed these men to use me, to take what they pleased without regard for my heart. Each fall into temptation was met with a wave of conviction, crashing over me like a storm, reminding me of the sanctity I had forsaken. What once ignited joy within me now left me hollow and sick to my core, a bitter reminder that pleasure devoid of purpose is a fleeting illusion.

I was caught in a relentless cycle, the weight of shame pressing down on me, as I wrestled with the realization that I had traded my worth for momentary affection. The deeper I sank, the louder the truth echoed in my spirit: love cannot thrive in the shadows of compromise, and I had allowed my desire for connection to blind me to the sacredness of my own being. It was a painful awakening, a clarion call to reclaim my boundaries, to rise from the ashes of my choices and embrace the divine love that awaited me—not in the arms of another, but within the depths of my own heart.

I felt the walls of my home closing in, the air thick with the weight of unfulfilled dreams and stifled desires. In search of liberation, I started skating at Venice Beach, gliding on the smooth pavement like a bird finally set free from its cage. The sun kissed my skin, and the rhythm of the waves called to my soul as I roller-skated under the vast expanse of the sky, where my spirit soared amidst the laughter and life of others.

But in the midst of this newfound freedom, I encountered a man whose smile was as enticing as the ocean breeze, a siren's call wrapped in charm. It was he who introduced me to the intoxicating allure of acid, a gateway that seemed to promise deeper truths yet beckoned me into darkness. I found myself slipping back into the embrace of old habits, the smoke of weed curling around my thoughts, tempting me to surrender once more to the ephemeral high.

Despite my fervent attempts to shield myself from the snares of temptation, I became a moth drawn to a flickering flame. With each lapse, each choice to indulge, I unwittingly threw open the doors to the enemy, inviting spirits into my life that danced on the edges of my consciousness, whispering lies that clouded my judgment. It was a heartbreaking realization—every time I thought I was merely seeking joy, I was, in fact, loosening my grip on the very essence of my being.

I felt the chains of my past tightening around me, each moment of weakness a reminder of how easily I could be led astray. The thrill of the skate faded into a bitter echo as I surrendered to influences I could not comprehend, allowing darkness to seep into the cracks of my soul. With every slip, I lost a piece of my light, a bright spark dimmed by the shadows of indulgence. I longed for clarity, for the strength to resist, yet found myself ensnared in a cycle that threatened to swallow me whole, drowning me in a sea of confusion and despair.

I stood at the crossroads of despair, feeling the weight of my choices like heavy chains around my ankles, pulling me down into an abyss from which I could not escape. Each day, I woke up wrapped in a shroud of regret, the echoes of past mistakes haunting me, whispering that I was unworthy, that I was weak and vulnerable—an easy prey for the insidious forces that lurked in the shadows, eager to exploit my fleshly desires. In those moments of despair, my heart cried out to God, a silent scream that reverberated through the depths of my being. "Why can't

I break free?" I pleaded, exhaustion clawing at my spirit, relentless in its pursuit.

I was weary, so tired of wrestling with the demons that danced around my mind, and the relentless cycle of shame that left me gasping for breath. "Why is this happening to me?" I questioned, my voice trembling with frustration and longing for answers. And then, in the midst of my turmoil, I heard Him—a gentle whisper that cut through the noise of my anguish like a warm light breaking through the darkest of nights.

God spoke to me, His voice a balm to my bruised soul, offering words wrapped in love yet laden with the truth I so desperately needed to confront. He reached into the depths of my heart, unearthing the wounds I had buried for far too long, those scars that had shaped me but had also shackled me in fear. The fortress I'd built around my heart dissolved and in that moment, my vulnerabilities were laid bare before Him, exposed yet held in the sacred embrace of His unwavering love.

With every word, I felt the walls I had built around my heart begin to crumble, and in their place, a profound sense of acceptance washed over me. His love was unfailing, a refuge in my storm, a reminder that even in my brokenness, I was worthy of grace. It was then that I understood—I was not alone in my struggle. God was there, weaving my pain into a tapestry of redemption, urging me to rise from the ashes of my despair, to reclaim the beauty of my spirit, and to embrace the strength that lay within.

Little Girl

Let me mend your wounds, my dear,
For I stand here, a promise wrapped in grace.
I am not here to inflict pain;
No, I call you to step into the light,
To rise from the shadows that have clung to your soul.
Your beauty deserves to shine, unencumbered,
It's time to unveil the masterpiece that is you.

I knew you long before your first breath graced this earth,
Sweet child, delicate and strong.
Your father knows the depths of your suffering,
The heartache etched in your soul,
And the absence of a mother's embrace,
That void, that silent ache.

Oh, God, I come to You,
Bearing a heavy load,
A plane full of baggage,
Each piece a reminder of my trials,
But I lay it all down at Your feet.
Take it, Lord, for it no longer serves me.

A new life awaits, shimmering on the horizon,
So be still, little girl, and trust in Me.

I promise you this: I will not abandon you.
You have never truly walked alone,
I have been your constant companion,
A silent guardian, guiding you through the darkness.

The light before me is bright, blinding,
Yet I hear Your call, God, sweet and clear,
"Come, little girl, step into your destiny."
And with trembling heart, I answer,
Here I come, ready to embrace the healing,
Ready to awaken to the beauty within me,
Ready to rise, to shine, to be free.

Focus on Me

I have wandered, distracted,
Caught in the snare of the enemy's schemes,
Off-balance, my spirit unanchored,
Not rooted in the sacred text,
Yearning for the Word, for it is life,
Yet losing sight, slipping away,
Power waning in the shadow of doubt,
Weakness wraps around me, heavy like a shroud,
Did I lose You in the noise,
Your presence feels like a distant echo?

"Focus on Me," the voice whispers,
"Not on the shadows lurking behind you,
For I have already claimed the victory,
And the closer you draw to My light,
The more the darkness seeks to pull you,
To cast you into the pit where it resides."

"Focus on Me,
Do not take your gaze from My love,
For I am your strength, your refuge,
I have called you home,
Into the arms of grace and redemption."

Conversations With The Most High

"Focus on Me; My grace envelops you,
Sufficient, unwavering, even in weakness,
For it is in the cracks of your spirit
That My strength pours in like a river.
It won't be easy, this path you tread,
But in Me, you shall find peace."

"Focus on Me amidst the trials,
These tribulations are mere whispers,
Trying to divert you from your destined journey.
Hold tight to the living Word,
Pray without ceasing, let your heart rise,
Endure, for the end is near."

"Focus on Me; dive headfirst
Into the depths of My unconditional love.
Marry Me, bind your heart to My purpose,
Trust the plans I have woven for you,
For I raised you up for a time such as this,
And never again will you carry worry."

Father

You are my Shepherd,
A guiding light, steadfast and true,
Like a loving father, You watch over me,
Correcting my course when I stray,
Redirecting my heart back to You,
Even in my blindness, I trust,
For You alone know what is best for my soul.
Surely, goodness and mercy
Will follow me all the days of my life,
A promise woven into the fabric of my being.

Tribulation after tribulation,
You stood by my side, unyielding,
Never leaving, never forsaking,
Leading me out of every shadow,
Not with harshness, but with gentle hands,
Loving me softly, sweetly,
Even when I felt unworthy of Your grace.

Oh, how I wandered, lost in the streets,
Desperate for love, an empty vessel,
Seeking to fill my cup with fleeting pleasures,
Yet all along, You were there,
A father's love wrapping around me,
From the very beginning to the end,
Embracing a runaway child with open arms.

Like a good father,
Your door stood wide, inviting,
"Come home, my child," You called,
"Let Me clothe you, feed you,
For the angels rejoice in heaven,
For you were once dead,
But now alive in My embrace,
You were lost,
But now found."

"Father, forgive me," I plead,
"I have sinned against You,
Make me Your servant,
And I shall serve You faithfully."

And then You respond,
"Child, weary and worn,
Come, I will give you rest.
Lay down your burdens at My feet,
I will renew your strength,
Prepare a table before you,
In the presence of your enemies,
Anoint your head with oil,
Pouring out blessings you do not deserve."

Yet in Your goodness,
You offer love freely,
You didn't have to, but You did,
And I will lift my voice in praise,
For the rest of my days,
Forever grateful for the Shepherd,
Who leads me through valleys,
And lifts me to heights,
In the arms of unwavering love.

I am

Here I am,
On my knees, humbled and raw,
Grateful for today,
For the breath of life that fills my lungs,
Each inhale a gift, each exhale a prayer,
A sacred dance between the seen and unseen.

Here I am,
Pouring out my heart,
Praying that You hear me,
For there are days when my faith rises like the sun,
But on days like this,
I feel unworthy,
A flickering candle in a storm,
Doubts creeping in like shadows at dusk.

Here I am,
The enemy assaults me, fierce and relentless,
I feel spiritually weak,
Yet I cling to the promise,
They who wait on the Lord shall renew their strength,
Like eagles soaring on the winds of grace,
Lift me, Lord, higher than my fears.

Conversations With The Most High

Here I am,
Help me not to stumble,
Not to move from the depths of my emotions,
But to discern and harness them,
For I long to know You,
To grow deeper in this bond,
For I simply cannot navigate this life without You,
You are the compass of my soul.

So here I am,
Order my steps, dear God,
Guide me along this narrow road,
Let my path be illuminated by Your light,
Here I am,
Offering my burdens to You,
Trusting that with each weight surrendered,
I am lighter, I am freer,
Cradled in Your everlasting love.

Taste And See

I have tasted and seen
That the Lord is indeed good,
A revelation that came as a sweet surprise,
Larger than life, filling every void,
For years, I feasted on the flesh,
Searching in shadows,
Yet craving the light.

And then, suddenly, I found I had ears to hear,
A heart awakened, a thirst for truth,
His mercy—my saving grace—
The Lord has carried me,
A mighty long way through the valleys of despair.

Listen to me now,
Sounding like the wise ancestors
Who sang hymns under the vast cotton sky,
Her spirit woven into the fabric of my soul,
For I have weathered storms,
More trials than many twice my age,
I am living proof,
Only He could have pulled me through.

My soul bears battle wounds and scars,
Each mark a testament to His redemptive story,

Conversations With The Most High

He never told me I was to play a leading role,
But as the tale unfolds,
I see His hand guiding every chapter.

What we fail to understand,
Is the depth of suffering and the weight of loss,
We ask, "Why me?" in our moments of despair,
But in the midst of it all, I read the back of a stranger's shirt,
It boldly proclaimed,
"Keep your head up—
God gives His hardest battles to His strongest soldiers."
Struggle builds faith;
Nothing happens by chance,
It's all part of His divine plan.

To shake you,
To break you,
To love you fiercely—
But He never forsakes you.
The Lord is good,
I have tasted and seen
That His unconditional love envelops me,
A warm embrace in the cold of night.

Following Christ means surrendering my life,
Taking up my cross day by day,
Seeking Him in the dawn's first light,
And the shadows of the night,
Reading His Word,
Yearning to know Him more,
Building a relationship on a solid foundation,
Brick by brick,
Let us not cast stones,
But rather flee from sin,

For we are all in the same boat,
Navigating these turbulent waters together.

Beloved, lend a hand,
Help one another,
So we can all stay afloat,
And together, we will taste and see
That the Lord is truly good.

Present

Here I am, time and time again,
In this sacred space, where we meet,
A hush falls around us,
Here is where we speak,
Where your voice echoes through the chambers of my soul,
Where I hear you clearly, cutting through the noise of the world.

Here is where you've always been,
Patient and steadfast, waiting,
I just have to pause, to catch you,
To breathe, to cease this frantic chase,
Running in endless circles,
Only to return, humbled, to this sacred place.

I thought I was heading somewhere,
Chasing dreams I deemed important,
Plans I crafted with eager hands,
Yet they crumbled like dust in the wind,
Lessons, it seems, disguised as ambitions,
Each misstep, a step back,
But here is where we start anew.

Here is where you teach me,
In the quiet, in the stillness,
Where the heart opens wide,
Here, is where I want to be,
Nestled in your grace,
Finding clarity in surrender,
And wisdom in your presence.

In this moment, I am found,
Rooted in love,
Awakening to the truth that I need not run,
For here, in your embrace,
Is where I belong.

The Lord Will Provide

To live in your presence,
Oh, what a blessing it is,
A gentle reminder,
That you provide abundantly,
Even when my pockets echo empty,
Down to my last $1.25,
Yet still, you cradle my heart with hope.

No room for pride,
When I can no longer hide,
No place for shame,
For you bear the blame,
Again and again,
Your love never fails, unwavering.

In the small things,
You reveal your care,
In the tender moments,
A soft whisper, a warm embrace,
And in the grand designs,
You show that you never forsake me,
Your hand guiding me through every trial.

The Lord will provide,
And yet, I question,

Conversations With The Most High

Why do I doubt?
I have never gone without,
Yet here I stand,
Wrestling with control,
You know me well;
You see my weary soul,
Tired of me,
Tired of this endless fight,
Tired of holding on so tight.

The toxicity I create,
Born of stubbornness and fear,
All because I refuse to let you be great.

Today, I choose to accept things as they are,
Surrendering my will,
Embracing the truth that life unfolds,
And in that acceptance,
I find solace,
And a peace that makes everything alright.

Conversations With The Most High

Jericho

As I gaze upon you,
I feel the chains gripping my heart unravel,
For you are the mirror of my soul,
A living testament to the journey,
The walls of Jericho tumbling down,
All that I once fled now pursues me,
Like shadows that refuse to fade.

When I peer into your eyes,
I see the little girl I once was,
The innocence that still hums softly,
Tunes of resilience,
Whispers of survival,
Each note a lifeline,
A melody crafted to soothe the night.

Surely, I must have been cradled by God,
Fashioned in the shadows,
And yet, I do not seek your comfort,
I long for your gaze to truly meet mine,
To recognize the beauty of my struggle,
To witness me in all my glory.

If you dare to look deep enough,
You will see yourself reflected back,

The echoes of your own journey,
As the walls crumble like Jericho,
A breakthrough born of courage and faith,
And in this sacred moment,

My spirit is vast, my voice soars as I walk with God,
a force greater than fear, a love deeper than any depth of darkness.
And I stand, unafraid.

About Bianca Avanti Rinehart

Born and raised in the vibrant, soul-stirring city of Atlanta, GA, Bianca Avanti Rinehart has always approached life with an adventurous spirit and a heart ablaze with passion. From the moment she could move, she was drawn to the exhilarating thrill of roller skating, a powerful escape from the hardships of a challenging childhood. Roller skating wasn't just a hobby—it was her form of freedom, her way of pushing past limitations, and of rewriting the narrative of her life.

But Bianca's journey isn't just about defying gravity on wheels. Though Bianca did not grow up deeply rooted in family values, she is now building and discovering these foundations through her own journey. While her early years were marked by a broken home, her path has led her to understand the profound importance of connection in all its forms. Growing up with a deaf brother, she learned early the power of communication and empathy, discovering ways to bridge gaps between people through understanding and patience. Her bond with her brother shaped her into a woman who recognizes that family connections can transcend traditional boundaries. In her late 20s, a serendipitous encounter brought her another brother, expanding her understanding of family and proving that love and connection can grow in unexpected places, no matter the time or circumstance. Today, she is intentionally cultivating the stable, values-centered family life she never had, learning and growing alongside her own children as she builds a legacy of love and faith.

After years of dismissing the possibility of having children while living a homosexual lifestyle it was God's divine orchestration through her brief marriage that she received the gift of motherhood and reshaped her understanding of family, purpose, and love. The journey of raising children became a powerful instrument of God's transformative work in her life, teaching her the kind of sacrificial love that mirrors His own. Today, she embraces the calling, recognizing that motherhood has been God's chosen path to deepen her faith and understanding of His unconditional love. She is building the stable, Christ values-centered family she never had, learning and growing alongside her own children.

As a devoted mother to two beautiful daughters, Bianca passed on the same daring, adventurous spirit that had shaped her childhood. It was in 2023, while roller skating with her daughters in a stroller, that she went viral, her infectious energy and the undeniable bond with her family striking a chord with thousands. That viral moment led to an unexpected honor: being featured on the cover of *LA Times Weekend*, a testament to her authenticity and her ability to inspire others with her vibrant, joyful way of life. To see her family's love and strength resonate with so many people was a humbling and heartwarming experience.

Roller skating has always been Bianca's passion, a lifelong companion that saw her through many phases of her life. Yet, in a moment of spiritual clarity, she made the courageous decision to step back from skating. This wasn't about giving up a passion—it was about realigning her heart and her purpose, embracing a new chapter that more closely followed the path God had set before her.

In addition to her love for movement, Bianca is a powerful rising force in the Christian rap and hip-hop community. She carries a gift of artistic expression that remained largely unexplored while she sought acceptance in all the wrong places. Her early life was marked by people-pleasing tendencies that led her down unexpected paths—including an appearance in a French Montana music video for $400, a decision that conflicted with her core values but reflected her desperate search for belonging.

Bianca translates her experiences into powerful, authentic art that resonates with those facing similar struggles. Her music and poetry serve as bridges between struggle and victory, doubt and faith, brokenness and redemption. Each piece of her work reflects the raw reality of her transformation—from a people-pleaser seeking validation to a bold artist living out God's purpose.

Every chapter of Bianca's story has been marked by courage, transformation, and a relentless drive to live authentically. Through her family, her faith, and her passions, she continues to embody the essence of resilience and purpose—facing each new challenge with boldness, grace, and an unwavering commitment to the life God has destined for her.

Through her unflinching honesty and artistic expression, Bianca inspires others to embrace their own journey of faith and transformation. Her story reminds us that our past doesn't define our future, and that the gifts God plants within us will flourish when we finally step into our true identity in Christ.

Made in the USA
Las Vegas, NV
06 December 2024